A SAM•U•L book
Copyright © 2013 by Sam Richardson

Illustrations by Sam Richardson

All rights reserved

Other books by Sam Richardson:
"Bite, Stings and Scratches: A Desert Journal"

"My Little Book of Caricatures"

"Taoseños, Terlinguaseños and Other Outlaws I've Drawn"

More on the author:
www.samuls.blogspot.com

ISBN-13: 978-1461171461
ISBN-10: 1461171466

Twelve
Lessons
of
the
Desert

by
Sam
Richardson

Twelve Lessons of the Desert
By Sam Richardson

Chapter One

Twelve months, twelve lessons, each lesson tied to a month of the year, each month its own season. My spiritual connection to the land and to nature and to the changing seasons of the Big Bend of Texas has been one of my greatest teachers.

It has been said that there are no mistakes, only lessons, and that the universe will keep providing you with lessons, one at a time, until you learn them.

It's true.

For each month I offer one lesson, some of my notes and observations from nature and a short essay—the products of journals I kept over a period of 17 years. Most of them were written in a little cabin I lived in down on Rough Run Creek near Terlingua. It's in the south part of Brewster County in the Big Bend country of far West Texas, not far from the Rio Grande.

I was a river guide there. River guiding is the educated man's alternative to the real world and the culturally bankrupt man's way to instant stardom. I did other things, too: edited newspapers, ran tours all over Mexico, wrote, sold art, made friends, made enemies.

Geographically, the Big Bend is a country with no fat. Emotionally and psychotically it is a state of mind, burnt on the backside of beyond. All that remains in the desert are geological bones, stripped bare by millions of years of erosion. There is a river and a few small mountain ranges, remnants of past habitats. And there is an independent race of hard-headed, self-sufficient people who have found a way to live in a region that is an unwilling partner.

Freedom has been my religion. The Big Bend lifestyle gave me that, the freedom to work and learn and travel at my own pace. But the independent operator, the free-lancer—in my case, river guide, tour operator, editor and free-lance writer—swims at the deep end of the pool. With the joy of freedom there have been times of doubt and despair, the product of working and living in a remote place with a seasonal economy subject to the ebb and flow of a dying river and rising gas prices and any number of other unpredictable, uncontrollable factors.

Nobody ever made any serious money in the Big Bend. That's not why people live there. Money creates relationships. You can never give it or receive without attachment and obligation. Most of us chose the alternative.

Some of my other tutors in the desert have ranged from sweet kind and loving people to unscrupulous mean and tortured souls whose madness tweaked my angry and competitive side and drew me into many a petty and insignificant squabble. I'm still not sure if the good people were as good as I saw them or if the bad ones were as bad as I thought or to what degree it was all a reflection of what I was putting out.

The severe Big Bend lifestyle can bring out your good side. And your neuroses.

Much of what I've gained—my lessons—has been learned time and again by generation after generation. Sages have said that there is nothing new except what has been forgotten. I've discovered a lot for myself, then realized that the wisdom was eternal and was there all along. It's just that I had to relearn it through the lens of the desert, usually the hard way by trial and error, then restate it in my own words. Some lessons were learned while observing the desert and all its citizens and seasons, others were only focused while living in the desert and thinking about my past experiences in other times and places.

I will keep learning. I probably should say I will keep trying to learn because, at times, in spite of what I know, I still don't get it right.

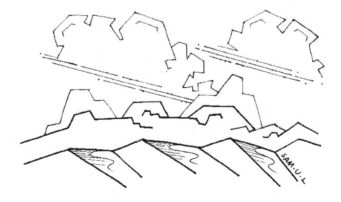

January, the Moon of Two Blankets

Lesson One: I will find something to be joyful about in each day and create my own rituals to celebrate it. I have everything I need. All I have to do is say yes.

January notes: January is the best month of the year in the desert. There's good weather and bad but for the most part we enjoy Indian summer days and good sleeping at night. It can get cold in January. And hot.

We look for bluebonnets the first few weeks of the year, some years finding them, some years not. Finding the first bluebonnet blooming becomes a treasure hunt and people report back where they've found a single bloom and that will draw a crowd, just one bloom. It will be tied to the amount of rain we had the previous fall: A lot of rain in September and October, big bloom; no rain in those months, few blooms.

Feathered dalea with tiny purple blossoms and bi-colored mustard with magenta and white petals are also common in January. In a good year, yucca start blooming in January and produce huge pods of brilliant white flowers.

Doves, sparrows, phyrrhuloxia, and cactus wrens are around. Ravens are year-round residents and always fun to watch. Later, the migrants and nesting species will show up.

January is the time for hiking in the desert and a good time to get home before dark on short winter days to curl up with a good book at night.

And January reminds us that there is always color in the desert.

A Winter Walk

There is a loneliness to the winter sun. The long, dark shadows of evening appear just after the noon hour, bringing an urgency to the close of day. When the light is gone, I like to go out and walk toward a January night.

In the darkness, things take on another dimension. As I move through the stillness, the rustle of my clothes echoes against nearby hills like limbs of a tree creaking in silent wind. The shudder of a startled covey of quail taking wing sounds for a moment like the low, rumbling growl of a lion. Off to one side there's the tinkle of gravel in an arroyo and, in an instant, something slides through a patch of light thrown by my flashlight. Coyote. Gone. Didn't even leave a shadow.

Winds whip ocotillo and mesquite back and forth

and tell every living thing to hunker down, get low, cover up. The biting cold of an evening connects us to ancestors who huddled against the earth thousands of years ago. I wonder what it was like for them when cold shadows covered the desert and the darkness of night froze everything to a halt. They would have heard the primordial howl of the coyote and wolf that proclaimed the natural order of those selected to survive.

Wolf is gone but from just across the arroyo comes the solitary wail of my associate, Coyote, the desert song dog. He reminds me that as the world changes, descendants of winged and four-legged and crawling ancestors will survive as they are and always have been while we, fragile creatures who get all the latest news from a satellite dish and engage in daily bouts of e-mail and text messaging, are moving closer to the edge. As our addictions to electricity, gasoline, computers and cell phones become more acute, we're getting closer to those other confused and complicated worlds we thought we escaped years ago when we moved to the Big Bend.

At least we still have these moments under the stars when all things and all days are the same. This is reason enough for celebration.

February, the Moon of Beginnings

Lesson Two: I will remember that life is a license to learn in public. I will continue to find things I don't understand and write about them. I read, I listen, I observe, I write things down. It comes out as a newspaper column or a book. Sometimes I get it right. Sometimes I get it wrong. Either way, people frequently disagree with me.

We all learn from the process.

February notes: Cottonwood and mesquite trees start to leaf out in February. Both will become major players as they grow: cottonwoods for shade and bird habitat; the mesquite bean will be a food source for a lot of my neighbors. We use the mesquite bean, today, to make an interesting jelly with its own personality. Native Americans ground them up and used them as a flour.

More bluebonnets appear in February and there may be a few early arriving spring flowers like desert windmill (a marigold) and some yellow composites. Of the latter there are many.

One February, we found a bluebonnet up in Ben's Hole Canyon that was over five feet tall. It had started blooming in November of the previous fall. It was, of course, a rare exception because it had taken root right on a spring which explained its unusual height.

Most Big Bend bluebonnets peak about knee-high at full maturity.

In some years bluebonnets not only line highways but blanket the hillsides. People will ask, "Are they seeded, does the highway department plant them?" We just point to the hills that go on and on to the horizon with their layers and shades blue and respectfully answer a question with a question. "Do you think anybody could have planted all that?"

At times, we see geese passing through in February. You hear them before you see them, look up and ... wow! It excites the mind to think about how they navigate and to wonder where they're going—Montana, Canada, Alaska, the Arctic?

One noon in February, a pretty rain came. Beautiful, wet, shining rain, a rare thing for the winter months. It subdued the dust and cooled the air and we were happy. But the whole thing lasted only a moment of a few hours. About five in the afternoon with clouds overhead and rain still falling, the horizon began to clear and the jealous sun came back to reclaim its desert. "No rain will stay here long," said the sun and as evening approached it made a grand exit, showing us all its color and brightness.

The next day, the rain was the talk of the town and a nice memory and the sun was back to work early.

Sometimes in February, spring will send an early post card of things to come. A hot, dusty windstorm will blow up, then we say, "Goodbye dear winter, we barely knew ye." In spite of the spring color and the tourist traffic yet to come, we'll miss the cool and tranquil winter days and all the time we have for hiking and reading and making art and reflecting. But we live in the moment, enjoying the last of the cool weather, not worrying about what's coming.

Slowly but surely the land is reinventing itself with the change of season. Great winds midwife the transition and howl across the desert at dusk each day, lifting clouds of dust. When things settle down at night, a million stars illuminate a cloudless sky. Each day may bring new color. First were the bluebonnets, then the yucca. Later there will be the magenta of pitaya and, in time, prickly pear with gradations from red to orange to yellow. And when the claret cup cacti blooms, with the brightest red the desert has to offer, we'll know it's spring.

Out on the river road, an antelope squirrel takes off up a talus slope and knocks loose a rock twice his weight. The rock, egged on by gravity, displaces other rocks and a small landslide crashes down to the road below. When it's over, rocks weighing twenty times as much as the squirrel lie in a cloud of dust 20 or 30 feet beneath places they've been resting for hundreds, maybe thousands, of years. And up above, El Antilopito, his small eyes sparkling like diamonds in the darkness, sits in the shade of a small crevice and smiles at his great power.

A little covey of quail, flying just a foot off the ground, rise along the side of a hill and light short of the top. As they scramble the last few feet to the summit, they set off a small avalanche of pebbles that cascade down with a tinkling sound like a gentle stone rain.

Two ravens locked in a dogfight glide across the desert, climbing and diving, changing directions in rapid movement. They make a lot of noise, cawing loudly. The chase goes on for almost a mile before the pursuer breaks off and lights on some old mining ruins. The next day, four of them duel in the desert sky. It's chaos and confusion as they weave an aerial web, trying to decide who's against whom. Finally the combatants scatter and light exhausted on telephone poles and mesquite branches. They eye each other and caw venom, each one trying to get in the last word.

A Desert Opera
Big coyote social down on Rough Run Creek one night. The starlit silence was suddenly broken by a high-pitched clamor. If you could give a visual color and shape to all the different sounds coyotes

make, the night sky would look life a great surrealist painting. When the song dog sang, I saw things spiraling, floating and shooting everywhere—an illustrated chorus.

Then, as quickly as it started, it stopped. Half hour later, a solitary descending wail curled out, wavered, dissolved and was answered by a sharp yip from a half mile down the creek. The wail ascended to a bark and the yip replied, repeating itself three or four times and moving closer. Then the yip and the wail ran together, were joined by others, and a new howling opera rose above the desert to join the moon.

When you heard them, it sounded like whole packs as the bunch came together to sniff résumés and hash out the pecking order.

In the morning, you'd find their tracks and could tell from the indentions in the dirt and patterns of little clods thrown behind that they were on the run, chasing something or chasing each other.

The sound was inviting and it was fun to think Coyote was having fun: the thrill of the chase, triumph of the kill, that sort of thing.

He's the perfect technician with all the tools he needs to survive in one neat package: the senses of smell, sight, hearing and the intuition to know what to trust and what not to.

When you did see him, he was a gray shadow in the night, blending in so well with moonlight that you'd see two forms, one real and one a shadow. They mirrored each other. The one on top had to be the real one—a silent, solitary hunter, always moving, always looking.

The desert provides plenty for those willing to work the terrain and even dig: jackrabbit, cottontail, kangaroo rat, antelope squirrel and mice for meat. And mesquite beans, persimmon and guayacon in season. During some weeks of the year, Coyote's scats indicate he's part vegetarian.

Some say coyotes mate for life but the legendary Texas writer J. Frank Dobie, among others, was skeptical of this view. Once he wrote, "In mating, coyotes seem a good deal like human beings: some are strictly monogamous and some are unstrictly polygamous. Some mated males, like many professedly orthodox husbands, would apparently relish more variety and less responsibility..." This is more in line with the Native American point of view—Coyote the scoundrel.

He was sacred in some cultures, sacred because of his imperfection. A clever trickster, the Indians called him. Through Coyote's folly, man was able to appreciate his own foolishness and develop a sense of humor. Coyote, according to legend, perfected the art of self-sabotage, getting himself in and out of scrape after scrape.

In the Big Bend where bighorn sheep, Mexican wolf and bald eagle were eliminated, and where the black bear was almost pushed out, Coyote hung on in spite of being hunted, trapped, poisoned and persecuted by the ultimate predator.

He's a clown, maybe, but one with a sense of timing the losers didn't have.

Just for one night, it would be good to be a Coyote.

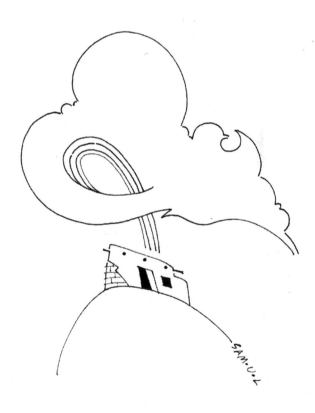

March, the Moon of the Good, the Bad, and the Money

Lesson Three: I will take what good things life and nature offer and remember that with them will come things I don't like, can't control but must accept.

March notes: By March, the battle is on. The desert comes alive and gives you all it has: wind, dust, heat, cold, spectrum ... tourists.

March is the busy season. Tourists, like the birds, return and for a few weeks we go crazy, trying to keep up with the demand for services: river trips, hikes, cook-outs, natural history seminars. But we get to share the desert with our visitors which is one of the rewards of life here. To teach is to learn twice. To me, the Big Bend has always the world's largest outdoor textbook.

March is make-it-or-break-it month for river companies, wilderness outfitters and guides. Make it in March or you don't make it. We work. We endure. We wonder how long our cycle will last.

New blooms on desert plant life bring the color and the excitement of renewal and the tourists bring the lucre that's necessary to survive in a region with a fragile seasonal economy, where nobody ever gets rich and where so many failed just trying to survive.

The second big bloom, the one everybody waits

for, is on in March. There are flowers everywhere in a wet year: Indian paintbrush, verbena, vervain, blackfoot daisy, purple mallows in the desert and along the river. Mexican buckeye in the canyons and madrone trees up in the mountains will have blooms on them, too.

Readers interested in plants and their seasons should pick up the books of Dr. Barton Warnock. He documented thousands of species in West Texas and several are named for him. His books are instant reference for the serious observer.

The claret cup cacti will flower in March. You'll see one solitary plant against the side of a hill, its vivid red blossoms calling attention to themselves like a beacon. The bloom is short-lived but worth traveling a few extra miles to see. Ocotillo produce a brilliant red flower and thick green leaves. Mesquite will continue to leaf out and show yellow tassels. Guayacon, a thorny affair with thin green leaves, brings small fragrant purple flowers and a lot of bees. Creosote, a.k.a greasewood, a.k.a. guamis, the most common plant in the lower desert, will flourish yellow flowers in March as well.

Vultures, the harbingers of spring, are back. They'll coast and soar all day for the next six months at least. They lose the thermals in winter and move south to warmer climes but, like the tourists, when they show up in waves, we know, if we didn't already, that it's spring.

Then there is the wind, the insulting wind. It kicks up in March. Even the heat and flies of summer are not as annoying as the March tempests that explode the dust and sting our hides beginning this month.

A Change of Season

A dust storm with scorching, howling winds that raged for hours seared us, one day. They burned and dried our hides and altered our moods. Clouds of dust hung in the air. It was hot and you could feel the pressure change.

The desert becomes a breathing oven sometimes and the processes of erosion get a boost as a layer of skin is peeled off both man and landscape.

Then everything clears off and, like an innocent child who never does any wrong, mother earth puts on a pretty face, feigns ignorance of past irritations and dares us to enjoy the day.

In spite of little storms and big heat, my neighbors stay busy. A cactus wren, like a street dog eyeing a turf poacher, stares at a dove that is getting too close. You can imagine a low growl as its head lowers. Then in a split second it thrusts its curved beak toward the intruder, sending the dove away in a flurry. Wrens are bold around my cabin and get into everything. Two of them were in my truck one day.

Doves attempt to mate with a lot of fuss and feathers. On my porch, an aggressive male tries to top an indifferent female. He flaps and rises above her, she screeches, moves and evades union and goes on feeding, which adds to his frustration and intensifies his rushes. Eventually, she flies away, out of range. "Not today, sir, not with me."

House finches check out the porchlight. They seem to be the most vocal of all the birds and a pair has made a nest in the light every spring.

As it gets warmer, I will have to start using a fan. Then the swamp cooler. Then, at times, nothing will help.

Vultures and wrens, doves and flowers, tourists and dust storms: springtime in the Big Bend.

SAM·U·L

April, the Moon of Howling Wind

Lesson Four: I will be in touch with my assets—my talent, my spirit, my energy—and act like I belong wherever I am. I've had a tendency to throw my body at most of my endeavors. Usually that's the best policy. Sometimes it's the worst. I refuse to change.

April notes: April has its own personality. Daylight savings has started, which gives the sun more leverage in its battle against our mortality.

I sleep outside a lot in April because my cabin holds the heat of the day a little too well and at bedtime the place is still warm. When I wake up in the morning, the air will be clear, crisp and cool and the temperature will be in the 50s. Two blankets almost aren't enough, sometimes.

As the sun comes up, the mercury rises into the 70s and my neighbors come out. Rabbit will be grazing on wildflowers. Dove, quail and other birds will begin their routines and recently arrived house finches will be starting their nest.

By early afternoon, the personality of the whole thing begins to change. For a time, the sun feels warm and good. You feel radiant with the heat but, after a while, enough is enough and you look for shade.

By late afternoon, the winds come and, with the heat, the place becomes a swirling inferno, uncomfortable and irritating. Hell in the afternoon: the price we pay for cool mornings.

Then the desert throws a fit and the winds deliver a long, screaming-hot blow. But by six or seven in the evening, most of the blasts die down and we're left with the boiling glare of the sun and temperatures in the 90s until dark, which won't come until almost nine.

Unfortunately, my cabin faces due west and I get the full brunt of the evening exodus. We've got five more months of this and it's going to get worse before it gets better.

The flies haven't even found us yet.

The Good, the Bad, My Quail and Mozart

The good:

Horses walk along it. Mule deer, javelinas, coyotes and lions, too. Their tracks mix with mine. I call it my mesa, even though it's not mine. Somebody else owns the property. It's not worth much, just a lot of rocks and cactus, but it's at a nice elevation where you can see things. I go up there almost every day and talk to the universe.

Millions of years ago it was a streambed. Water found a level there which explains why so much loose rock is spread over the top of it. It took a lot of water to move all these rocks. When the stream withdrew, erosion dug deep and exposed what was below it— clays and limestone, the remnants of ancient seas— and created a little badlands, brightly colored yellow

and red and gray, uneven and rough cut with arroyos
and creeks. Sitting above it with a view of the Chisos
to the east, Mesa de Anguila to the south, Lajitas and
Terlingua to the west, and Bee Mountain to the north
is my mesa.

I do a lot of talking up there. Heavenly Father,
Mother Earth, Grandfathers of the Universe, hallowed
be thy names. Don't know who's listening but I talk
anyway. Sometimes I feel the presence, other times
I'm not sure. But talk is good, even if you just talk to
the wind. Clutch at the wind, count the dust. I get a
lot done up there.

The bad:

Dust is eternal. Ashes to ashes, dust to dust, never
ending, perpetual dust, remnant of all civilization and
geography. It's the beginning, the end, the relocation
and the rebirth of everything.

Dust, the vanguard of erosion, leads the charge
to new territory, usually in my living room or porch.
I have a temporary arrangement with the planet and
live in a cabin near a creek in an area of a desert. The
dust, however, does not recognize this "deal" and
reserves the right to cover and cake over everything
in my world. We have a never-ending debate about
land rights. My small victories are ephemeral and
have to be won over and over again.

Dust lies sleeping in winter. Harmless powder,
benign veneer of the landscape. But in spring it
awakens and like an angry predator, starved and

annoyed by a long, draining hibernation, transforms itself into a howling monster intent on reinventing the region and everything in it.

Fortunately these tantrums only last a few minutes or hours a day and only occur during a few months of the year. Then, like a seasonal migrant, it shows itself briefly and becomes an ethereal creature, exploding, soaring, sweeping through the territory, bent on leaving its mark. It has a life of its own and connects us to this desert—another reminder of our mortality.

My Quail and Mozart:

Then when the wind subsides and the dust settles, my quail reappear. Like royalty they march to Mozart. From somewhere behind me, my jam box purrs the master's music, the perfect background for an afternoon parade as my quail look for seeds and bugs and water. The perfection of the music orchestrates their dance and color. They glisten blue against the side of an arroyo, their movement an evolving pattern. There is a grace to them, each one a subtle hallelujah to the music of a master.

SAM•U•L

May, the Moon of the Flying, Crawling, Scratchy Things

Lesson Five: I will not divorce my friends when they side with people I disagree with on civic, political and religious issues, at least as long as they haven't sided with an enemy against me.

I'm reminded of the old saw which says my brother and I will fight among ourselves, my brother and I will fight my cousin, my cousin and I will fight an outsider.

I see this in nature. House finchs fighting other house finchs for territory, then banding together to fight black-throated sparrows for turf, then house finches and black-throateds teaming up to chase cactus wrens out of the neighborhood.

I've learned you can like people you don't agree with—or even trust. In the end, I'd like to have a few friends, people I can laugh with.

May notes: Lot of nighthawks around. They compete with the bats for the evening feast of flying bugs. Mockingbirds, black-throated sparrows, vermillion flycatchers and green-tailed towhees are back and can make meals out of dark black loteberries that grow on a thorny bush.

Mesquite beans are green and getting fuller. Whitethorn acacia in front of my place bud in May and the creosote bushes produce a fuzzy seed.

I sustained an invasion of flying ants in the house one May evening. I couldn't figure out how they got in and couldn't keep them out. Then, when I turned off the last lamp and they couldn't find light, they sought heat and kept crashing into the lampshade, after which they found something else warm to crash into—me. One got into my ear and before I could do anything it got right up next to my eardrum and started making a high-pitched screaming sound. Scary! I thought about what would happen if the thing got excited and bit my eardrum so I flew to the bathroom and poured alcohol into the ear. That put a stop to the screaming.

They came back again the next night but I was able to keep them out of my ear by leaving the cabin to them. I went outside to sleep. Next day they were gone.

A day or two after that, I scored the first confirmed kill of the season—smashed a fly that lingered a little too long on the front screen. It was the first of many thousands to die in the never-ending battle of summer—man against the heat and the biting, stinging, scratchy things.

Up on the porch at the Terlingua Trading Company in the Ghost Town, the porch sitters and beer drinkers will be passing out flyswatters to all who attend the daily sunset watch.

That brings to mind the words of a great Terlingua philosopher who, whilst imbibing there among the swatter-armed and dangerous porch crowd, said, "Don't kill 'em all, boys, leave some for us to kill at home."

One day in May, there was a big lizard fight out in front of my place. Two titans of the dust got it on in a rustle of pebbles, mesquite beans and thorns. Right across the front of my cabin they went, then around the side of the porch and up a small incline before they disappeared into an arroyo. It all happened in just a few seconds. Relative to their size, it would be like two boxers running at full speed, trying to hit each other, occasionally whirling around and making contact and covering a ring the size of about two football fields.

Lizards seem to glide. You wonder if they make contact with the ground or just ride a cushion of air. They must be the fastest critters in nature, certainly for their size.

Every year, house finches nest in my porch light. It is a gawdy Spanish-style thing with decorative ironwork underneath that forms a hollow space just the right size for a nest.

They average two or three eggs a year. About half the time a generation of baby birds appear. Maybe half of those make it to flight school. Some years the cactus wrens spike the eggs and dash them on the ground, sometimes the babies fall out of the nest, sometimes ants get them.

And then there's that first and only attempt at

flight. Fly away or glide safely to the ground and there's a chance of survival. The alternative is fatal.

I dang near performed an incandescent lobotomy on a mother bird one time. When I have a guest nester, I don't use the light as long as they're there but once I forgot and turned on the porch light one evening about ten. A few minutes later, after I'd gone inside, I heard something bouncing around outside. When I heard the flutter between thumps I knew it was a bird of some kind but why was it doing a kamikaze mission on my porch, flying into everything? A second later, she landed on the screen door, evidently attracted to the light in my living room, and just hung on for a minute, shaking, looking around, finally looking right at me as if to say, "What in bloody hell are you trying to do   to me?"

I guess that must be quite a sensation, having a giant light about ten times the size of your head and bright enough to blind you fire up an inch above your face, especially when you had no warning and didn't know anything like that even existed. The heat must have been intense.

I turned out the light.

Lechuguilla is one of the indicator plants of the Chihuahuan Desert. Its curved leaves rise about a foot from the base of the plant and end in a sharp spine. They grow in clusters making it difficult to travel in areas they dominate. Cowboys call them "shin daggers" for good reason. The flowered stalks of those bloomed out to full maturity bend toward you in the May wind like lonely coyotes wanting to be petted. Like the century plant, they only bloom once, then die. But the old plants will spread plenty of seeds and will be replaced with a new generation soon enough.

First yellow blooms on the cholla cacti up in the Chisos Mountains are visible in May. Goldeneye, a shrub-sized plant with spiny petals, and yellow bells are starting to bloom. Yellow bells are also called trumpet flower because their blossoms are trumpet shaped. Locals call them esperanza, too. Sweet-scented desert willow and whitethorn acacia also come into flower.

The century plant, one of the marquee players in the desert, start to mature. It has its own myth which says it only blooms once in a hundred years. True, it only gets one bloom but it comes when the plant is closer to 20 years old. It blooms, distributes its seeds, then ... muerto. When the cycle starts, the stalk, which looks like a giant asparagus at first, shoots up, growing as much as a foot a day. When it reaches its peak, it throws out its arms, they flower, then go to seed. The big plants in all their brilliance look like giant radiant candelabra.

By late May, a female house finch is on the nest.

The male makes regular appearances and feeds her. I kind of cheat nature by putting out a lot of scratch around the place so the finches and everybody else don't have to work quite so hard. I always have a lot of customers. In addition to finches, there are sparrows, doves, cowbirds, quail and antelope squirrel, that I see, and probably a lot of other varmints at night, which I don't see, that take advantage of the free feed.

I caught a tarantula hawk one night. They're beautiful giant wasps with phosphorescent blue-black bodies and long graceful brown orange wings that extend out over the tail. Their long legs are attached to the trunk of the body and a couple of antennae originate from the V between the eyes. I put it in a quart jar and studied it for a while, made some sketches, then took it outside and let it go.

Sometimes during the day, I lie down in Rough Run Creek for a few minutes, my back hard against the baked clay. Then you can feel the sun and look into the limitless sky, feel the fullness of the heat and see how long you can take it.

Not long.

But when you feel it and embrace it, it becomes part of you and helps you deal with the physical and psychological price the heat extracts.

At night you can walk comfortably along the roads and in the desert wearing only mocassins and shorts, being careful to carry a flashlight so you can see where you're stepping.

Bluebonnets about gone by May and the ocotillo are dropping flowers but if there has been sufficient rain, they store it in their thick, green leaves. Century plant, lechuguilla and sotol are sending up stalks. Goldeneye, desert willow and acacia catclaw are blooming. Catclaw and desert willow are fragrant.

Turf wars. Black-throated sparrows, building a nest on the other end of my porch from the house finches, attract some attention. They nest in a small hole just big enough to get through on the underside of the roof. The hole leads into a dark hollow space about six inches deep, which is formed by a crossbeam between the roof and a layer of paneling.

Cactus wrens are curious devils and assiduously harass the sparrows. The wrens can't get in the hole because their bodies are too wide but they can hang upside down by their feet on the rim of the hole and poke their heads in. When they do that, the sparrows pitch a major fit, squawking and fluttering, trying their best to distract the wrens.

Black-throateds don't lack courage. One or two that were squabbling over territory minutes earlier will unite against the wrens and attack, being careful to withdraw just in time to avoid the wren's long, sharp, curved beak. Cactus wrens are also bigger so a fight would be a mismatch. Eventually the wrens go away and the sparrows get back to work on their nests and to fighting among themselves.

And one year, right in the middle of the porch, halfway between the house finches and the sparrows, an ash-throated flycatcher made a nest in one of my old cowboy boots that I'd hung from a beam, just for decoration.

Finches, wrens, sparrows and flycatchers. More fun than watching TV.

May is also a good month for boating. Most months are in the Big Bend, assuming there's any water in the river, which isn't always the case, but May is one of the last months of temperate weather before the oppressive heat of summer sets in.

I got into river guiding as I approached middle age, which is when most guides are getting out of it. This passage from one age to another, from the type of work I'd been doing (media, advertising, teaching) to wilderness guiding became one of my greatest adventures.

Of Boatwrecks and Learning

"Go for the hole and dig," Buck says.

I tighten my lifejacket, check to make sure all my gear is lashed down securely, take a breath, start for the rapid. I'm alone in the raft. The water is up. It is my first training trip. My education on the Rio

Grande begins.

A hole is a small chasm in a river rapid with an unrelenting current at one end that drives you toward a wall of water at the other. Hitting the hole is like hitting a brick wall. Everything stops for a split second with a deafening, tidal crash. Seems like forever when you're in there and it's got you. What happens in the next moment is critical and almost entirely up to the boatman. If he doesn't take action or hasn't positioned his boat properly, the river takes over and there's usually some sort of small disaster.

Sometimes a major one.

The river is up, swollen, raging. Every creek and arroyo is discharging thousands of cubic feet of water, the runoff of recent rains. Puffs of clouds spot the sky like tiny puffs of smoke left from the storm that exploded across the Big Bend last night.

A 14-foot Hopi rubber raft floats the river like a cork, especially with only one person and very little gear aboard. Rafts need a little weight in big water— gives them stability. Too much weight makes them hard to maneuver. No weight makes them unstable. Small boat, little weight, big water, green boatman: formula for disaster.

When I hit the hole, the front end of my bobbing little craft is sucked under water and stopped cold. When the rear end catches up with the front end, the raft doubles up, then the wave that forms the wall at the end of the crater begins regurgitating the boat.

As the raft emerges from the far end of the hole, it springs back to life, becomes airborne, inverts. I'm ejected, crash into the river. The boat comes down on top of me and its middle chamber, where I was sitting a few seconds ago, forms a dark, watery coffin over my head. I can't see. I can't breathe.

Quickly, I duck under water, emerge in the river, see daylight, breathe, clear the water from my eyes. Floating around me and slowly drifting away are plastic bags containing frozen fish and steaks. Boxes of rice and pancake mix are soaking up water and starting to sink. Utensils and plates are already at the bottom of the river.

Buck is showing very little concern for my well being at this point. He's pulling food out of the river as fast as he can. I think I hear him curse. I finally grab a bowline, pull my boat ashore, right it, reconfigure, resume rowing downstream. Now I'm even lighter.

We continue down the river, make camp, things settle down. The customers laugh and talk about my boat wreck. They think it's funny—what an adventure. Buck gets control of himself and serves a decent meal under the circumstances. He's professional and knows how to adjust but he never looks me in the eye again during the trip.

The next day, I'm an instant celebrity in the boating community. Word of a boat flip spreads across the area like a virus. Everyone revels in it. They say there are only three kinds of boatmen: Those who haven't flipped but who will, those who have, those who will flip again. And those who have love to hear about other people's wrecks.

But from these wrecks we learn, if not from someone else's experiences, from our own. I should have been told what to do when I hit the hole. Before that, I should have been told to stay out of the hole. I could have just as easily skirted it, stayed dry, avoided catastrophe. I didn't realize that was an option. I thought boating was supposed to be a dangerous adventure. Listening to the other guides talk, you might get that impression. But boating is as dangerous as you want it to be. Or as safe.

My education on the river began that day.

I never had another boat flip.

Postscript: My fellow guides ragged me endlessly about the wreck but I made hay with the incident and had the last laugh.

I turned this piece in as part of my course work when I was working on my masters at Sul Ross State in Alpine and, as a graduate student, was invited to read it at the annual meeting of the Western Literature Association, an association of college educators. I was probably the oldest graduate student at the meeting and appeared to be older than most of the professors in attendance. The piece was also published as one of my regular newspaper columns for a Big Bend weekly.

All that from one boat flip.

June, The Moon of the Slow, Hot Swelter

Lesson Six: I will remember that circumstances are the result of choices. And we make the choices. There will be days when it's best to take inventory of what you've got left, not what you think you've lost. And I'll try to remember that what you lose will sometimes come back if you're patient and don't burn bridges.

June notes: Now begins the siege. Summer surrounds us with tranquil layers of heat, one heaped upon another the other until the temperature reaches 100 degrees fahrenheit everyday. From noon until eight or nine in the evening, we sizzle and give thanks each evening when the sun sinks below the horizon. My cabin will absorb enough heat to be unsleepable at night. When you lie up outdoors, conenose beetles, spiders and scorpions can get at you—maybe not every night but just often enough to set you chanting prayers for winter as you implore the universe to speed up the passage of time and bring on a new season.

We remember: We chose to live here.

Lots of birds around. Eggs incubating, adults maintaining turf. Major aerial combat between several house finches right outside my window one afternoon. A couple of extraneous females tried to check out the nest in my porchlight and were attacked immediately by the resident couple. Both male and female evidently were watching from a nearby tree and when the intruders came they were instantly set upon. After the invaders were dispersed, the male got on the nest to check it out. He actually appeared to be counting the eggs. Then the female climbed back in and sat for a while. She hadn't been sitting with that much regularity lately, maybe because it's hot already.

Black-throated sparrows are an aggressive species. I've seen them literally at each other's throats locked in what seemed to be the ultimate struggle. No one dies but the losers vacate the territory quickly. It's mainly fluff or, in this case, bluff—bluff and feathers.

The dove is an interesting critter. The symbol of peace is actually aggressive and territorial. They will tolerate smaller birds and let them share feed but they won't tolerate other doves and they're constantly flushing each other off their feed with kind of a growling sound.

At times, though, there are some interesting moments of sharing. Once I watched a black-throated sparrow feeding another, apparently a younger one, on the ground. The younger one was sitting in the middle of some feed I had put out but had not figured out how to get it off the ground. The older bird scooped some feed up and fed the younger one.

Mesquite beans are on the ground by now and turning yellow. They'll be food for a lot of neighbors. Javelina will eat them. Rodents will store them for year-round use and in lean times coyote will eat them. I walked up to within a few feet of a coyote with a mouthful of mesquite beans once. I guess the crunching was making so much noise that he didn't hear me coming. Coyotes usually don't let you get that close.

June is now or never for my house finches. In all the years I lived in the little cabin near Rough Run Creek only about half of the eggs hatched and only a small percentage of those fledglings made it out of the nest.

Evening tempest is still a regular event. Not to be outdone by earlier spring months, June can produce a good blow and send anything not tied down airborne. One lesson I never seemed to learn was to shut all my windows and doors if I left the cabin in the evening. Storms could rear up suddenly, blow through, soak everything then disappear in a short time. And they could emerge from a clear blue sky or sneak up from behind the Chisos Mountains like a street dog waiting to attack.

Then when I'd come home, I'd have a lot of yard art—blankets and mattresses and chairs and anything that wasn't tied down had been blown off the porch, soaked and covered with a thin crust of mud.

Usually after one of those little environmental episodes, the desert would be singing the next morning. There might be a thousand birds, trying to outdo each other in song. I always wondered where they went when the blow was on.

Up in the Chisos, century plants, like giant flaming candelabra, are in full bloom and ignited with color. In wet years, eagle claw will produce a few short-lived blooms in June and there may be some late-blooming pitaya.

Lot of lizards like the whiptails are in the neighborhood and they attract roadrunners which are always amusing to watch. Skinks, a bigger type of lizard, make a pretty good living on my porch in summer where they find plenty of spiders, crickets, grasshoppers and beetles, all of which they're welcome to.

Summer Dance
Vultures caught aloft in a summer dust storm are twisted and turned and whipped like spastic kites. Trying to level off, they turn away but the tempest at their backs hurls them forward and they fight to gain altitude to avoid smashing into trees, poles and barns.

With the force around them, it's not even possible to land. Wings and tendons and joints are stretched to the limit. They'll be sore tomorrow.

Sitting at a public house in Terlingua, sipping a beverage with a friend, we watch the vulture kite olympics and talk about the problems of life in the desert during the summer: the heat, the dust, the bitin' bugs, no work. How do we do this year in, year out, we ask each other?

Right in the middle of the conversation, a tourist walks up, introduces himself and says, "I envy you guys living here. This must be the life."

A stunned silence for a moment. Then my friend and I look at each other and break out laughing. Laughing hard.

The tourist moves on and we finish a beer and watch a thunderstorm just off in the distance. Real storm, not just wind and dust. Dark clouds and lightning bolts on the horizon. There's the low rumble of thunder. The storm snarls and prowls like an angry cougar circling our camp, occasionally spitting a few rain drops in our direction, never coming too close, .

Get out your flashlights, boys. The power usually goes out when the wind kicks up. Power poles topple, lines break. But we need the rain.

Summer. We dance.

Some drawings

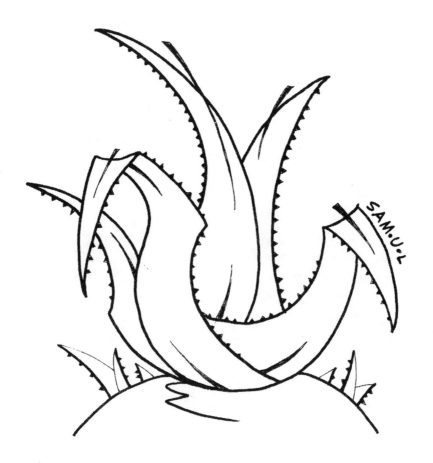

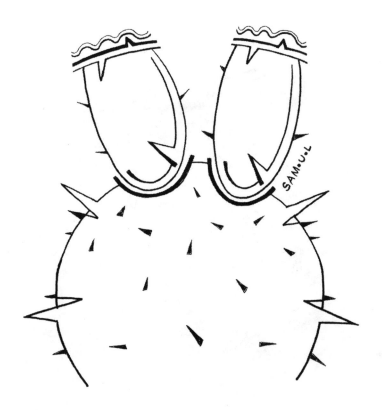

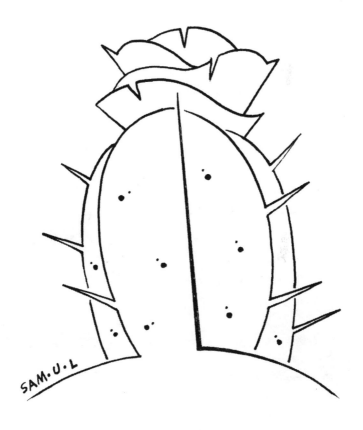

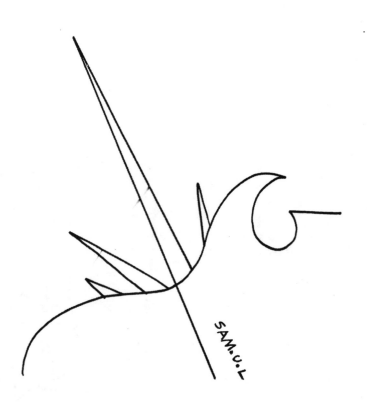

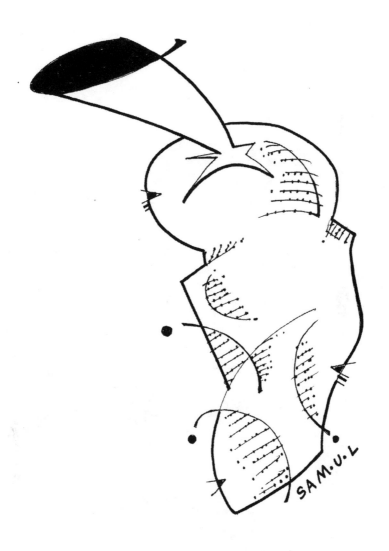

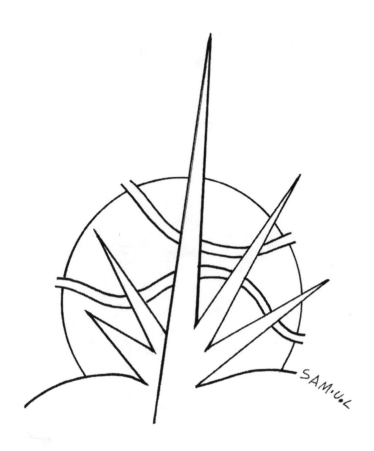

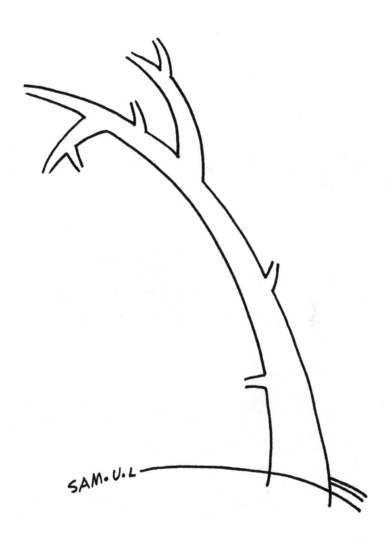

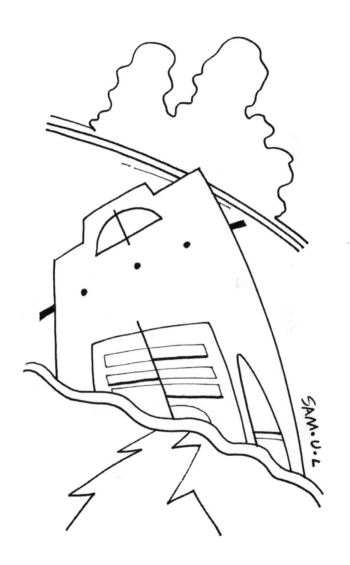

July, the Moon of the Unhurried Air

Lesson Seven: There's not enough room in my mind for anger and remorse, even though I frequently made room for them—many times and to my regret. If I hadn't, I wouldn't be human. It's me against me on that one. The battle continues.

July notes: In July, we endure, we abide. No new blooms. Mesquite, acacia, creosote and cottonwood are hanging on to their leaves. Creosote turning that yellow green color, getting dry and pasty.

Raven sitting on a telephone pole, proclaiming himself. This has become a daily ritual. I sometimes talk back to him: "What's your problem, what are you talking about, who do you think you're talking to, you're just in love with the sound of your own voice." He babbles on, probably just in love with the sound of his voice.

The heat continues. Up to 100 degrees everyday. By now we're used to it. The only thing that was—I say WAS—making life bearable was that most of the bugs were gone in July. But that changed.

We didn't used to have mosquitoes, but thanks to people who damned up creeks and runoffs, creating standing water that quickly grew stagnant, and gracias to other people who left old tires lying around (they collect water), we got skeeters in the new century. So much for sleeping on the porch.

Sleeping outdoors was never without its perils. In June, cone nose beetles are out and if you don't really lather up with repellant, they make a living off you— the same beetle—for days. They are bloodsuckers and anesthetize an area, usually on your leg, take a draw, then leave a dime-sized welt that itches like hell for days. I got tagged 14 times in one two-day cycle and had to take Benadryl and go soak in San Soloman Springs up at Balmorhea just to get relief.

Another time, I got stung twice in one night by a scorpion, the same scorpion I think. They are everywhere. I've killed as many in the house as outside. Got bit solid on the ass one time when I was sleeping indoors. There's nothing you can do to get rid of them. They just ARE.

Few Rufous hummingbirds about the place in July. They make a loud buzzing sound. Some people call them "buzz bombs." Your first reaction at the sound is that they're huge bees or wasps and you tend to reach for a swatter, until you see what it is. Sometimes they just fly through the porch. Zing! Incredible how fast they're going.

Three Ears, a cottontail, hung out with me one summer. I named it such because its left ear was split. Looked like something shredded it. Three was pretty skittish, even for a rabbit. Any sound, any movement—boom, gone. Just a gust of wind would set it off and running. Other cottontails around the place were a little more docile. Some would even have a lie down and relax from time to time—as much as a rabbit can relax.

It's not unreasonable to hope for rain in late July and in most years we get it. Something about the rain lifts my spirit. Love a cloudy, cool, overcast morning. Rough Run Creek, just a few hundred yards from my place, roars when we get a good runoff. Frogs are a symphony at night.

Last of the house finch fledglings make the big leap by mid July.

Little blue-gray gnatcatchers flitting around the bottom of creosote bushes. Delicate little birds with long, black tails. They know their place.

Big hail storm one July. Hard rain with hail blew in sideways from the north just after midnight and sent everything on my porch asunder. Didn't do much for the paint job on my truck, either. From searing heat and dry creek beds one year to rain and hail the next, you never know what will happen in the desert.

A Summer Walk

Walk down an empty road into a dark July night.
Climb a hill, stop, sit.
Watch.
Wait.
Listen.
Feel the darkness.
Wear the heat like a hair shirt.
Move on. Use your flashlight. Rattlers about.
They're moving slowly and when you step up to one it
just lies there and flicks its tongue at you. Never seen a
human before. Too hot to get excited. They wait until
you walk around them. Don't even buzz.

Nighthawks and bats work the unhurried desert
air and find plenty of bugs.

Haven't seen much of my neighbor Coyote as
of late. A loner wails every now and then but there's
no answer.

The star nation sparkles overhead.

Evening storm did a lot of damage. Spurges and
other plants with shallow roots were ripped loose,
turned upside down and left to dry out and die in
the sun.

This time of year the weather is fickle. Every other
day or so about sundown, the enervating, slothful
heat turns into screaming wind and rain that appears
in just a few minutes and races at you from a distant
horizon. Everything that's not tied down gets shredded
or blown to kingdom come. Then, like a bad child, the

disturbance disappears into the sunset and the desert puts on a clean, innocent face.

Go home, curl up, get in front of a fan, start a new book.

First light of morning brings duty raven, soaring overhead. Wake up call. Turkey vultures take up stations on telephone poles and spread their wings like great icons. "Behold," they seem to say. "It'll be hot again today."

Summer.

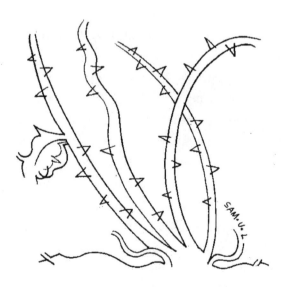

August, The Moon of Rains When It Can

Lesson Eight: It is a falsehood of the ego that I am an important person and have to be treated in certain ways. I look at what we endure in the Big Bend summer and realize that there is no security or guarantee of comfort or endorsement in nature and that we know and accept that. So what's this with your ego telling you somebody didn't treat you with respect? Respect is self-respect. Ultimately you don't have anything to prove to anybody but yourself.

August notes: Historically, August was a good month on the river. Summer rains in Mexico flushed the Rio Conchos which fed our part of the Rio Grande. We looked forward to big water and a little excitement running rapids. We would sometimes get water from the upper Rio Grande, generated by snow melt in Colorado and New Mexico.

But by the change of the century, increased irrigation in both the United States and Mexico, invasive species like the salt cedar and carriza cane which began to take disproportionate amounts of water, and with unpredictable drought cycles, our part of the stream became a dying river.

We were dragging boats across mud banks and gravel bars a good deal of the time instead of rowing over them in normal water or steering over them in big water. And as the water got lower, the boats were replaced by canoes that were rowed up river for short stretches instead of down river in long stretches.

Horses always know first. Like living weather vanes they turn and face the wind. Nostrils flare, manes and tails whip back.

Clouds hang a dark curtain across the horizon. From somewhere in the distance, thunder crackles like a string of firecrackers set off all at once, then rumbles, rolls and echoes across the Chisos Mountains. It ends with a deafening crack. Everybody and everything gets quiet.

The power of nature in these moments is frightening, transcending.

Then, a shower. Future historians won't compare each thunderstorm to Noah's flood. But for people who live close to the land, each little cloudburst has meaning.

When it happens, we write about it and talk about it for quite some time and compare it to other downpours. Then we'll file all our stories and drag them out next year and put them in perspective when it rains again, which is about how long it can be between downpours—as much as a year.

Big rain usually brings the river up. Then everybody in Terlingua will then make their annual trip through Santa Elena Canyon. And if we can get the word out, more tourists might show up to punch the big water. If the water holds, the river companies will have to summon the troops back from New Mexico and Colorado to do the work. In real dry years, guides get enough of boat draggin' in low water and go north to find steady work and tackle the whitewater.

There were times when I probably rowed as many river trips in July and August—when we had steady water—as I did during spring break. But that was then.

Like an old rancher said, "A little rain cures a lot of things."

One of the highlights of August is the blooming of cenizo. There are three species in the Big Bend: One will blossom with magenta flowers, another produces a dark purple bloom and another will flourish white. Their aroma is intoxicating. Just to walk through a patch of them and take a deep breath is a high. They don't always bloom every year and sometimes they'll produce in one area but not in another, just a few miles away. Depends on how much rain runoff they get. But in a good year, they're everywhere.

One year we had a plague of moths. Hundreds of them—many hundreds—would light on my ceiling. Everybody else in the area had them, too, which meant there must have been millions of them around.

The only way I could get rid of mine was with a hand-held vac. I would scoop them up, never getting them all, but I could get most of them. The next night hundreds more would appear. The plague lasted almost a month. We never knew why. There was nothing we could do about it so we experienced it, then were glad when it was over. And it only happened once.

At other times we'd have a rash of flying ants and biting flies. They say when the flies start biting it's going to rain but that's not true. Flies bite for most of the summer but it doesn't always rain.

Roadrunners like to play. Saw one chasing some rabbits, once. Three or four were grazing between some bushes down by a little gully. Roady would chase one, then the other. They didn't seem to fear him because they wouldn't run very far but they do jump if there's any movement nearby so Roady was taunting them to get a reaction. Another time, I saw him teasing a small flock of doves. Same game: He'd lower his head and charge into the flock, dispersing the lot. Great fun.

The way rabbit's head in constructed he has almost a 360° range of vision. His eyes are on the side of his head so he can see on either side, in front and, with the exception of a small patch, behind, too. When he turns his head just a little, he can cover that patch as well, which gives him 360° vision. Good vision, big ears and the ability to reproduce rapidly—the tools of survival.

A big blue heron circling the place one late August day. I took that as a good omen. Herons lead us down the river when we're out on the stream. This day, he led me in a circle, then disappeared.

Circle, circle, look, wait, be aware. Some of the best things just happen.

Big Water, Good Water

Good to be back on the river again. Big rise came through last week and cleaned everything out. Estimates were that it got as high as 12 feet, running as much as 10,000 cubic feet per second: Big water, good water.

Three of us boarded Gray Dog, a 16-foot, oar-powered rubber raft, at Lajitas. We were bound for Santa Elena Canyon. No hurry. We didn't get on the river until eleven. At high water levels, you can make the 20-mile run in three, maybe four hours. Normally, it's an all day trip.

The river was running a rich brown, the color and almost the consistency of chocolate milk. Lots of debris floating around. The Rio takes care of its own housekeeping at these levels and flushes its banks, leaving them clean and slightly—sometimes greatly—rearranged.

I love the anticipation of a river trip when the water level changes. It's like visiting a place I've never been before. There's a sense of renewal.

Half hour after put-in, we hit the first rapid,

Matadero. Bam, we ran it. Not much of a splash.

It was actually a little washed out but there was enough of a hole to get us wet. At some levels Matadero has a boat munching hole that can invert your rubber chariot. I know. They don't call it Samadero for nothing. Ancient history. We rolled over it, no problem.

Around noon we arrived at San Carlos Creek, just outside Santa Elena Canyon. It was cranking and spewing dark water the color of a Hershey bar, water even darker than the Rio and there were noisy boils and waves where the creek coiled into the river. Take one river, add one creek at flood stage: Big water.

Last year, a vaquero tried to ford this spot during a rise like this and drowned—both he and his horse. It's no toy, the Rio Grande.

A few minutes later, we entered the canyon. The sense of awe you feel in that chasm is indescribable and we were transported, both figuratively and literally. Not only were we inspired, we were picking up speed. The same amount of water that we'd been riding on the Rio had been juiced up by the flow from San Carlos, then compressed into a much narrower space between the walls of the canyon. Same amount of water, half the space—we were truckin'. And just around the first bend was the Rock Slide, the Big Bend's biggest rapid: Apprehension.

The Rock Slide: A maze, a boulder field of house sized rocks that fell into the river in some bygone era. It's an ever-changing puzzle, different with each rise and fall of the water. We eddied out and climbed scout rock to see what we were dealing with.

What we saw were boils, eddies, standing waves and holes, cooked up to a gnarly chocolate froth that culminated in two big pouroffs at the bottom. Just a few feet to the left of the pouroff on the Mexican side—where we needed to go—a big log had lodged itself on top of Clamshell Rock. One jagged end stuck out like a dagger, intruding on our intended route—a little extra challenge to add to excitement to our run: Adrenaline.

We decided to go right (Mexican side) anyway, log or no log. Center pour-off (Texas side) looked flippy. No point in going swimming at that point if we didn't have to.

Smooth run, no problems. Somewhere under us, under all that roaring water, was the Mexican Gate, Center Slot, Dog Nose, Space Capsule and Pillow Rock. We pushed over them pretty fast. Part of the Dog Nose was showing so we went to the right of it, cut back to the left, then hard to the right to avoid getting sucked into the Slide's angry center. Then there was another move to the right and the nose of the boat kissed the boiling water above Pillow Rock before we pulled into an eddy. Go to the left of Pillow Rock and you're in the belly of the beast. After a brief pause in the eddy, we punched the pouroff on the Mexican side, being careful to stay away from the log on top of Clamshell Rock.

A pouroff is like a little waterfall that ends in a violent hole. Everything that goes into it comes back out and takes a slap at you. The boat must have disappeared for a minute when we hit the bottom. The wave at the end of the hole came up over our heads, stopped the raft with a deafening tidal crash and we side-surfed for a second. Seems like forever when you're in there and it's got you. It's like hitting a brick wall, bouncing to one side, then resuming speed—a split second unraveling in slow motion, a small forever.

Then we were through it and rubbing our eyes. It felt like a handful of sand had been thrown in our faces. There was a lot of silt flushed from the banks in that new water.

Afterward, we pushed downstream and from there on out the canyon the water was steady—fast but there were no more rapids. The 1500-foot walls of Santa Elena towered above us like a cathedral and as the boat turned each bend of the river more surreal limestone shapes appeared ahead. Far above, hawks and vultures rode the thermals and just overhead dozens of smaller birds darted back and forth, going about their business. Some things are eternal.

The Rio Grande took thousands of years to cut its way through this wilderness. It has given life and it has taken it away. It has been the main landmark in an isolated territory claimed by the Spanish, the Apaches, the Comanches, the United States, Mexico, bandits, bootleggers and businessmen.

Now we're here. Someday, someone may write a little chapter about us, then file us away with all those who were here before: History.

Count us lucky.

September, La Luna de la Cascabel

Lesson Nine: Sometimes it's best to just sit and observe and let the universe arrive.
Observe and exist.
Be aware.
The brilliance of autumn, the gray of winter, the energy of spring, the sloth of summer, the movement of the sun, the moon and the stars.
Plants, animals, birds, colors, shapes, sizes.
Breathe.
Understanding will come in its own time.

September notes: Snakes move in September, especially rattlers. We see them along the highways. On the other side of the Rio, they're called vibora de cascabel, the viper with the little bell. Wherever rattlers live, early fall is the time they probe their territory and take care of all their business. And they buzz more when you move near them, especially the blacktails up in the Chisos Mountains.

Blacktail is a fighter and competes for his territory, coiling up in defiance with a snap, then a constant buzz when you come near. I always yield.

Down at the lower elevations the diamondbacks are more docile. They freeze when they sense activity and you can easily walk around them or even step over them.

Rattlers are out more when there is no moon.

They're sensitive to heat so they don't have to see. No moon, no light, they have the advantage because they sense their prey's body heat but their prey can't see them.

For us that means the cardinal rule of hiking in the desert at night is to carry—and to use—a flashlight at all times.

A few cenizo may still be out in September, with late bloomers just opening up. Yellow bells are still blooming as are desert poppies with their bright orange petals.

We may get a cold snap in September. Then, after all the months of relentless heat, our moods improve and the pace of life quickens. It'll be hot again the next day after a cool night but each day the thermometer drops a degree or two and we start getting weaned from our swamp coolers and fans.

Wild persimmons are dark and ripe and edible. Cottonwoods starting to drop a few leaves. Yellow butterflies still about. There will usually be some rain and the creeks will rise and fall, going from swollen raging little tsunamis to totally dry overnight. We sometimes see an eagle claw cactus blooming in September, a rare treat. One specimen near my porch sometimes gave me one bloom for just one day and that was it for the entire year.

There are unpredictable cycles of insects this time of year. In some years there will be grasshoppers whose wings are colored a bright red on the underside. One year we were visited by a swarm of flying green bugs that survived a tenure of one day. They were followed by flying ants who stayed for a time, then disappeared. Birds do well when the tiny crawling, flying things appear.

In September we anticipate fall and winter, the best months of the year, and we step gently around migrating rattlers.

A Feast of Days

Sitting on my porch eating cold melon and fish. The sun melts into the western horizon, taking the heat of the day and a little bit of the summer with it: Closure.

The limitless sky is cooler each night as the season changes. Light of the moon—a Comanche moon—and a million stars illuminate the desert: Brilliance.

By day, a hundred shades of green are complemented by the red of penstemon, purple of mist flower, magenta of cenizo, orange of desert poppy and yellow of dozens of composites: Spectrum.

The sunsets become more restful in September. Soon, there will be good sleeping outdoors in the autumn air: Balance.

At night, I like to take my jam box out into

the desert and play Comanche songs under the stars. There's a haunting, dangerous sound to the ancient's wail. I dance, being careful not step on a diamondback or scorpion: Spirit.

A hundred years ago, the old Comanch' would have gutted my ancestors for treading on these sacred lands. A hundred years from now, our spirits will soar here together: Eternity.

The full, rising moon passes overhead and stands vigilant over the western horizon, waiting for the return of the sun: Universe.

A butterfly—mariposa—lights nearby and looks at me. He has only a few days. I have a few years.

Same difference.

Some of this limestone around here is hundreds of millions of years old. Fathom a hundred million years.

Impossible.

Me and the butterfly. We have a moment—a few hours, a few days, a few years.

Same difference.

No difference.

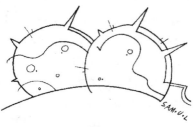

October, the Moon of the Floating Mountain

Lesson Ten: It's OK to be myself. Everything that has happened in the past brought me to the present moment. All was prelude to what will happen in the immediate and distant future so I will avoid extreme makeovers to accommodate other people and their systems. Most systems are failures anyway. Ultimately, only the individual can succeed.

October notes: A caterwauling coyote set up one morning not a hundred yards from my front porch. He was a weird one. Just sat there and barked at civilization, usually at about dawn. My neighbor's lazy pack of hounds across the road wouldn't even answer. Maybe that was the problem—coyote wanted to argue and nobody would give him the time of day. This one had an unusual bark, preceded by an indescribable twisted wail but mainly it was just a bark.

It wasn't that common for a coyote to just sit there and bark and to do it like it was barking at something.

I thought it was fussing at me and thought that it might be rabid so I sent a shot in the dark to scare it away. But it came back and I heard it a few times after that and think it was just on its own kick. If it was rabid, it survived a long time in that condition. More likely, it scavenged an old hippie camp, got into some garbage and scarfed down a leftover acid tab.

Most blooms gone in October. Snake weed,

maybe some jimmy weed seem flush. That's about all. But the weather continues to turn cooler and there's always the possibility of rain.

With the change of season, the desert becomes invigorating in the morning. It's a good feeling to get a cup of coffee and, with your shirt off, go out on the porch and feel the crisp new air on your skin. The October light takes on a special quality. There seems to be more of a glow and translucence early in the day and in the evening there's a magenta tint to everything.

Late-blooming cenizo sometimes add a spark to October. Guayacon show pretty red berries. Yellow bells and goldeneye are still in full flower. Limoncillo bloom.

With cooler weather and occasional rain comes ground fog that is especially beautiful around the Chisos Mountains which seem to float on it. That is part of the old saying about the Big Bend:

The Big Bend country is where the rainbows wait for rain

Where the river is kept in a stone box

Where the water runs uphill

And where the mountains float in the air, except at night when they go away to play with other mountains."

—*Unattributed*

Ravens of Autumn

Four ravens sit on the side of a hill with their backs to the evening sun. In the fading light of an autumn evening they glisten like black onyx. To lift off they have only to spread their wings and the wind raises them into the air. Then it's play time: rising, falling, circling, cawing. The force of a brisk wind keeps them aloft. Facing into the tempest, they hover almost motionless. Turning their backs to it, they shoot forward on extended wings. Changing angles, they circle and soar, dive and glide: An aerial ballet.

With autumn, the weather and colors of the desert change and we remember why we live here. Layers of heat that built up to form the anvil of summer slowly begin to float away and the land softens and breathes.

The harsh light of the summer sun bleaches rocks and mountains, buttes and mesas. There is contrast but little color. Now, with arrival of fall, the spectrum broadens. Mountains glow magenta in the evening light, distant mesas become subtle, slate blue shapes that lie against the horizon and the luminescence of October light adds warm pinks and glints of orange to compliment cool blues and purples. Our spirits are awakened from summer hibernations. We're renewed, reinvigorated.

There may be a late bloom on the cenizo. Magenta blooms will engulf the plants and drip from the branches. And from out of the blue, four ravens swoop down and glide over the bushes as if to bathe in the glow of desert color for just a few seconds.

Fall is a good time to be in the Big Bend.

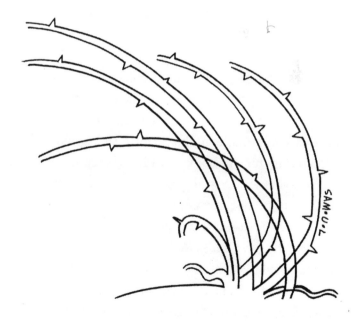

November, the Moon of Yellow Leaves

*Lesson Eleven: I will remember that it is better
to be a late bloomer than to have bloomed early and
faded. I see plants blossom ahead of their normal
season after a rain, only to be snapped off by an
unexpected freeze or be taken by a flash flood. But I'm
reminded that their seeds are eternal and there may be
ocotillo in October and yellow bells in November when
their expected bloom is months earlier. Either they've
flowered late or blossomed again after an early-season
peak and it reminds me that in the face of all failure
and disappointment I should be patient and try again.*

*A famous artist once said that the only way to fail
is to quit.*

November notes: When the cold shroud of winter
lowers itself onto the land in November, much of
the desert starts falling asleep. Sporadic winds whip
ocotillo and mesquite back and forth and seem to tell
every living thing to hunker, get low and cover up.
Winter's in town.

Mesquite, acacia whitethorn, cottonwood, and
creosote still have leaves. A few random blooms
still throw a little color in November: Apache
plume, limoncillo, blackfoot daisy and butterweed
in the desert and mist flower, with a pretty purple
blossom, up in the Chisos. Little yellow, brown and

yellow-green butterflies hover around the mud near waterholes. There are black and orange grasshoppers that make a clicking sound when they fly. Many times I've heard that first "click" and and jumped, thinking it was a rattler. "Gotcha again," says Grasshopper.

Big grasshopper set up housekeeping in my front room one time. Pretty to look at. I had a little brown snake in the house for a while, too. After I checked to make sure it didn't have any bells on its tail I left it alone. Guess it found something to eat. It was welcome to anything it could swallow, especially if it moved. Maybe it got the grasshopper.

November mornings are cool but the temp can rise into the 80s of an afternoon. Summer hasn't totally let go but 80 is easy compared to 100. And we've had snow as early as November. It will melt by noon but it's a great change, almost a spiritual high.

Lot of roadrunners around. They make an interesting sound that starts with a "hooo," then tapers off into a clicking reverberation. The clicking is their beak, which they snap together dozens of times a second like a castanet.

I saw three of them together one day. They were strutting and dancing around each other in some sort of game. One had a lizard in its beak that it seemed to enjoy showing off. Roadrunners parade a bit when they catch one, even if nobody but me is watching. It's a classic image: roadrunner with a limp lizard dangling from his mouth. Chow time!

For the Big Bend community, a small society rooted in two countries and two cultures, the Rio Grande was just a technicality, something that got your feet wet as you crossed back and forth. People from both sides of the river traveled to either side at will. That changed with 9-11 but, before that, we had a lot of fun in Mexico. I remember one November night when three of us ventured down to San Carlos for the annual Fiesta.

Saturday Night Comancheros

The thunder seemed to come from the earth beneath us that morning. We felt it first, then heard it, a distant roar. Little by little it was getting louder.

The night before, we'd attended a big baile in San Carlos, Chihuahua, Mexico, just 17 miles south of the Rio Grande and, afterward, had looked for the first quiet, isolated place to throw our bedrolls down.

Following a rutted track south of San Carlos, we drove a short ways until we couldn't hear any more barking dogs or see any houselights and stopped in what seemed like a good spot. There, we piled out of the truck and hit the ground like a sack of rocks, all three of us. None of our small troop of Saturday Night Comancheros was more than a few feet from where the hissing old truck was parked. Sleep had come quickly under the clear November sky and we were oblivious to the wide open ranch country we'd just driven through and the small mountain range just ahead.

As the eastern horizon started to glow, the promise of warmth from the morning sun was still a few hours away so we drew up tighter in our sleeping bags and tried not to think about the hard, cold ground we were stretched out on ... except it was vibrating with a steady, pulsating roar.

I finally jacked myself up on one elbow and tried to concentrate. The sound was coming from the east and I could see a cloud of dust rising from an arroyo not too far away in that direction.

The early light of day was illuminating the desert around us by that time and as I began to focus on our little impromptu campsite I realized that we had thrown down right in the middle of a stock trail—a well traveled, frequently used stock trail.

When I rolled over and looked back to the west, I could see some Colorado-colored mountains that had been a dark shadow the night before. A small canyon cut them through and where the canyon exited the mountains a small stream had gathered into a big waterhole. The trail we had been sleeping on led right to the water.

"Cowabunga dudes!" I yelled. "We've done camped right in the middle of a horse freeway and ever' caballo in northern Chihuahua is headed right at us. It's too late to save the truck, every man for himself!"

Getting out of a tight-fitting, zippered mummy sleeping bag is not something you do in just a few seconds. You wear a mummy bag and sometimes they don't let go so easy. Zippers get stuck and clothes get hung up but there wasn't time for all that. The only thing to do was try to get up and move in the bag the best way we could.

The site of three tightly bound polypropylene caterpillars with human heads hopping across the trail and into a cactus patch may have slowed the herd down a little—a few shied off to one side or the other—but most ploughed through our hardscrabble bedroom like a snorting hundred-legged locomotive and kept heading for water.

When the dust had cleared, we held a quick roll call. Everybody present and accounted for and, by that time, completely awake. No serious injuries and not too many cactus punctures. Sleeping bags actually give pretty good protection if you've got to go hopping through a cactus patch. The remains of a pair of boots that had been lying in the trail resembled a leather dog bone a Rottweiler had been chewing on and the truck looked like a piece of outdoor sculpture, covered by dust the color of the desert.

We sat there for a minute, then started grinning and kind of looked at each other with that look that says, "Hot dang, son, we nearly 'bout squatted on our spurs again."

"Hola, amigos. Buenas dias," the vaquero who'd been driving the horse herd said as he rode up. "You gringos are pretty funny, camping in the middle of a trail."

"Yeah buddy, anything for a laugh. Hope we don't owe you nothing for camping in your backyard."

"No sharge, amigos. We gonna have a lotta fun telling this story for a long time."

December, the Moon of the Enchanting Dark Sky

Lesson Twelve: If you can't make peace with the past, change the story. Cast yourself as the hero, not the victim. It might have been you in that happy ending and you just didn't realize it.

One way or the other it will become less important as time passes.

December notes: Igneous intrusions, exposed by eons of erosion, looking like the skeleton of the earth, protrude through hundred-million-year-old marine sediments. There is the sense of timelessness when you consider the age of this landscape. And spread thinly over the bony surface of the desert there is life ... and change.

Mesquite leaves are turning yellow and starting to drop. With the leaves and the beans, which turn tannish yellow, there will be a blanket of gold around the mesquite. Cottonwood leaves turn a golden color as well in December, then drop. Guayacon, acacia and creosote will still be green but have lost all their flower and fruit. Feathered (or bearded) dalea will flower.

Time to give nature another assist by putting out a little bird seed. Pyrrhuloxia, house finches and sparrows hanging out in the feeder I put on the porch. Sparrows, doves and quail who seem to get along will take advantage of another feeder I set under a mesquite away from the cabin.

Camelot

We all have our Camelots, those sweet spots of childhood we've sanitized and redesigned to fit a picture of the way we wish things had been.

I remember sitting in church on Sunday mornings, listening to my Father's sermons and I recall a favorite hymn the choir and congregation would sometimes sing: "There's a church in the valley by the wildwood, no lovelier spot in the vale/ No spot is so sweet to my childhood as the little brown church in the vale."

It all seems like the little brown church in the vale as I look back on it. But I also remember a lot of it wasn't that great at the time.

My gang always sat in the balcony on Sunday mornings, our small act of rebellion. Since we really didn't have a choice about going to church, we could at least sit together and away from the rest of the congregation.

And being the preacher's kid had its pressures, too, which added to my personal insurrection.

"That preacher's boy is a wild one," they'd say.

Not really, but he was a rebel. Still is.

"How sweet on a clear Sabbath morning, to list the clear ringing bell/ Its tones so sweetly are calling, oh come to the church in the vale."

Sweet remembrance is calling—now—but at the time we would play hooky from church whenever we got the chance. Never got away with it but every kid growing up has to devote a certain percentage himself to fighting the system. I fought hard and viewed life as a battleground where coming of age was a struggle. It was no Camelot.

King Arthur's Camelot was supposed to be a magical, mystical place where lived chivalrous knights and honorable ladies. Everyone belonged and life made sense—at least that's how we use the term "Camelot." But the Arthurian legend is more of a myth.

There probably was an Arthur Pendragon (King Arthur) but over the centuries writers like Alfred Lord Tennyson and Sir Thomas Mallory added the rest of the cast and what they might have been like. The real Camelot, had there been one, would have been a very human place and less than perfect.

In the actual story, Sir Lancelot and Sir Tristram were involved in illicit and destructive affairs— Lancelot with Arthur's wife. Arthur himself was born out of wedlock, was denied by his father and, in the end, died at the hands of his enemies. With all that infidelity and violence, why do we think Camelot was such a neat, happy place?

Because we want it to be, that's all. That's how we choose to use the term. History and legend are sometimes just a fables agreed upon and so the Arthurian legend has dissolved into sugary mythology—sweet remembrance of a tragic opera.

It's no sin that we do the same to ourselves. We learn to love things we've suffered for and eventually realize that there were good times hidden in those confusing, sometimes painful days. We wouldn't mind reliving some of those times and do in memory but we make a few corrections and additions as we go over the territory again. In the end it turns out right.

And when you stop and look around, everything can be OK in the here and now. Camelot is in attending to the details of daily life, in taking care of your home and your things, in the love of family, in satisfying conversation and silly talk with genuine friends, in learning and teaching, in good food, in walking through the desert and inviting your soul, or just sitting on your porch and just ... sitting.

You get to write your own legend, then live it.

"From the church in the valley by the wildwood, when day fades away into night/ I would fain from this spot of my childhood, wing my way to the mansions of light."

Where you find Camelot is not as important as when.

And when is now.

Postlude:

I got into river guiding at age 45, the age when most guys were getting out of it. The fact that a middle-aged guy with a gray beard could do anything a 20-year-old could do triggered some insecurities in the younger dudes but we adjusted to each other.

I used to joke that, like the younger bucks, I could row a river trip, down a couple tequila shots, drink a six pack, then plan, pack and load the next day's trip and get up the next morning and row it—but, in my case, not in the same 48-hour period.

They could do it all, day after day.

With me it was row the river, couple beers, good supper, early to bed. Then row the river, day after day. I saved the six packs and tequila shots for my days off.

In the Big Bend:

I renewed my interest in classical music. Chopin, Beethoven and Mozart seemed to complement the eternal landscapes of the desert much better than rock 'n roll. And jazz became a comfortable compromise when I didn't feel like rock or country on the one hand or the classics on the other.

Pure silence was even a better choice.

I came to the conclusion that there is as much evil in the world as there is good but in spite of some people's insufferable habits and manipulations everybody on some level means well.

I learned to let myself be kidded and realized that sometimes your faults are what other people like about you. Those little flaws are often what bind us together.

I learned that what happened is irrelevant. What people think happened is what you have to deal with.

I discovered that you can't win them all but six out of ten is damn good.

I learned something about patience. Didn't always practice it but I learned that when I was patient, things worked better. Walk softly, be nice and people may do things your way. Sometimes they have to think it was their idea but if they're part of the process things go better. Hitting people over the head with your ideas and telling them what you want and what you think is best seldom works.

I learned that as a guide and interpreter that as many visitors as I entertained over the years, few remember my name or exactly what I said but most remember how I made them feel.

I learned that bad things will eventually happen to me. And they will happen again. People will treat me poorly. And they'll treat me poorly again. The question became not why did these things happen, it is what did I learn? What will I do the next time?

I learned that it's OK to get mad. Mad at yourself, mad at events, mad at people. When things go badly, I will try not to react, I will try to detach myself emotionally and try to observe, first, and see what the universe can provide. The universe will have its way, anyway. We wait.

I learned to leave the decline of my enemies to themselves. They get what they deserve which is not always what I think they deserve. And I still hold out hope that when I get what's coming to me that I will like the result.

I learned that some of my heroes were people I didn't like. They were people who lived off the grid, who built their own houses and carried their own water and renovated hopeless old buildings to start businesses that met the unmet needs of the community. They were hardheaded, fiercely independent people who did things their own way in their own time. Because of their resilience and determination and ability to survive they earned, if not my affection, at least my respect.

By learning where I was, I learned more about who I was. There was good and bad in both cases. The trick was always to look for the good and abide in it.

And I learned that in real life, the rules are seldom simple ... or fair.

Deal with it.

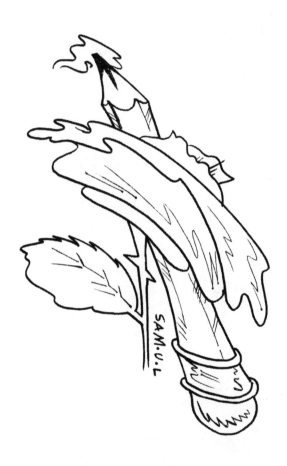